Talking Myself Home

Talking Myself Home

My Life in Verses

Ian McMillan

JOHN MURRAY

First published in Great Britain in 2008
by John Murray (Publishers)
An Hachette Livre UK company

1

© Ian McMillan 2008

The right of Ian McMillan to be identified as the Author of
the Work has been asserted by him in accordance with the
Copyright, Designs and Patents Act 1988.

A CIP catalogue record for this title is available from the
British Library

ISBN 978-1-84854-045-3

Typeset in ITC New Baskerville

Printed and bound by Clays Ltd, St Ives plc

John Murray policy is to use papers that are natural, renewable
and recyclable products and made from wood grown in
sustainable forests. The logging and manufacturing processes
are expected to conform to the environmental regulations of
the country of origin.

John Murray (Publishers)
338 Euston Road
London NW1 3BH

www.johnmurray.co.uk

For Catherine, Kate, Elizabeth, Andrew ...
and Thomas

Contents

Introduction: Just a Few Bones

Mine is a small life that's happened in a big century.

I was born at 34 North Street, Darfield, near Barnsley, on 21 January 1956. My family, my mother and her mother, my brother John, who was born in 1948, and my dad, who was away at sea at the tail end of a long career in the Royal Navy that began in 1937, all lived round the corner on Barnsley Road but because my dad was away my mother decided to have me at the house of my auntie and Uncle Charlie. She wasn't my real auntie, of course.

I was born into a place that seemed settled; nothing much happened in our corner of the world. Most men worked down the pit and the women either worked in factories or mills or in the pit canteen or they stayed at home and looked after the kids. The pit dominated the landscape, the huge stack of Houghton Main taking up quite a section of the sky.

My dad was from a place called Carnwath, not far from Lanark in Scotland; he and my mother met as pen-pals. My mother was from Great Houghton, the next village to Darfield, and her mate had a pen-pal on my dad's ship. Her mate (I think her name was Molly) asked if there were any other lonely sailors who wanted to write to Yorkshire girls and the epistolory romance began. They wrote to each other as the war began and met occasionally, and got married on a forty-eight-hour pass in Peebles (where my dad's family had moved) in 1943. My mother, who by this time was in the WAAF, and was stationed at RAF Blackbrook in Lancashire, was refused leave and so went AWOL. On her return she was arrested. Arrested for love.

My dad left the navy in 1958 and went to work for a firm of architects in Sheffield, leaving the house at the same time every day and spending his spare time fishing and tying flies. I was lucky enough to go to a West Riding County primary school, under the great Sir Alec Clegg, a chief education officer who insisted that all children were creative. Low Valley Junior School made me who I am and, more importantly, instilled in me the belief that everyone is creative and that everyone can improve their creativity. Teachers like Mr Moody, Mrs Hudson, Mrs Roche, Mr Manley, Mrs Hinchliffe and many others, and the West Riding County Library at the bottom of Snape Hill, helped to make me the person I am.

I left Low Valley Junior and went to Wath Grammar School; somehow, in that summer between schools, I made up my mind to be a writer. I obsessively borrowed and reborrowed a book called *Writing For Money* by Harvey Day. I read and wrote all the time: handwritten historical epics with names like 'The Rise and Fall of the Lokan Empire' and James Bond-lite stories starring Jaz and Big Shelley. Big Shelley was actually a bloke who walked past our house every day but I thought it was a great name for a secret service agent. Jaz was his glamorous assistant, loosely based on Emma Peel from *The Avengers*. At secondary school I was encouraged by a teacher called Mr Brown, who introduced me to the work of Ted Hughes by giving me a copy of *Crow* and saying, 'Here's a book of jokes: it'll make you laugh.' I wrote the kind of tortured adolescent verse that people write at that age and I got it published in the school magazine. I started going out with the girl who has been my wife since 1979.

I wanted to perform in public and with my mate, and future brother-in-law, Martyn I formed Oscar the Frog, a folk-rock band. I was the world's worst drummer (perhaps because I only had Tupperware, not drums, for the first few weeks) and I soon got the sack, as did Martyn. But I'd been bitten by the bug of standing up in front of an audience, and, looking for places to perform our poems, we went to folk clubs and read our deathless verse; we eventually created a poetry/comedy/folk act called Jaws, which spent endless evenings in upstairs rooms in pubs all over the north of England.

After Wath Grammar I went to North Staffordshire Polytechnic to do a degree called Modern Studies. I travelled across America on a Greyhound bus with my mates Dave and Bob, and I wrote and read. I was starting to get poems published in magazines.

I graduated from North Staffordshire Polytechnic with a 2:2, which shows that I'd been writing too many poems. It was 1978 and I was determined to become an author. The trouble was, I didn't know how. I wasn't earning any money from my poems and I was about to get married, so I went to work in a building site. My first booklet, *Batteries Not Included*, came out in 1980, as did my first book, *The Changing Problem*, published by Carcanet. I was invited to give occasional poetry readings, and Jaws was getting the odd paid gig. I was sacked from the building site and I took a job in a tennis ball factory. It was 1980 and I'd been married for a year. The odd gig in response to my books still came my way but it was harder to find time to do them because I was working shifts. I decided to give it all up and become a writer.

I applied to Yorkshire Arts in 1981 for a grant; at that time they would give you up to £1,000 if you went freelance. They awarded me £800, which isn't that much less but psychologically it feels a lot less. Luckily my parents and my wife were very supportive (my wife was working as a teacher at the time) and I packed up in, I think, May 1981.

Since then I've been a freelance writer and performer and broadcaster and I'm unusual because I've stayed in the same place; I still live about half a mile from where I was born. I'm still married and we've got three children and, at the time of writing, one grandchild. My dad had a stroke and after several years sitting in a chair, died on Christmas Day 2001; my mother died on 4 January 2007. This place has changed now: the pits have all gone, the old certainties have become uncertain, the landscape has been greened over, although I still walk down to the same paper shop for my paper.

But I'm still convinced of this: words are important, and everybody can create them.

The verse autobiography that follows is partial; there's plenty there, but there's a lot left out. Enjoy it. And then have a go at writing your own.

04/01/07

The telephone shatters the night's dark glass.
I'm suddenly awake in the new year air
And in the moment it takes a life to pass
From waking to sleeping I feel you there.

My brother's voice that sounds like mine
Gives me the news I already knew.
Outside a milk float clinks and shines
And a lit plane drones in the night's dark blue,

And I feel the tears slap my torn face;
The light clicks on. I rub my eyes.
I'm trapped inside that empty space
You float in when your mother dies.

Feeling that the story ends just here,
The stream dried up, the smashed glass clear.

Closing the Door: A Few Facts

She came back from the dead twice;
The doctor said she'd be gone within the hour
And that she'd be dead in 45 minutes
Or that she'd start to come back.

These are facts. I don't like facts much.
I find them slippery fish that change as you hold them
And they try to splash back
Into that facty sea they came from.

Facts. Keep 'em. Stuff 'em. Fuck 'em.
Chuck them back in the sea where they belong;
Just leave me with this fiction:
After 45 minutes she opened her eyes

And looked at a picture of our grandson Thomas,
Just a month or so in the world.
And she smiled and said 'Beautiful.'
And he is. And you were.

Two-Line Smile Poems about
the Houses I've Lived In

34

Opening my eyes for the first time here
I smiled at the wallpaper, I'm told.

108

I buried pebbles painted gold in the garden;
I told Mr White next door I'd found gold. He smiled.

13

We'd sit in silence in the front room, smiling,
As Holin Hammerton practised the piano next door,
    swinging.

79

We smiled, that first night. Then we watched
Singing in the Rain on a tiny black and white television.

9

I drew a smile in that spilled flour. Then I sneezed;
I looked like the ghost I'd be some time. Still living here.

The Facts

I've mythologised this thing so much
That I've lost sight of the reality of it.
Think of the sea, bucking like a pulled rug.
Think of the land, holding like glue.

John, my dad, in his cabin, writing
Those letters that told the whole story,
That were the story.

Olive, my mother, in barracks, writing
Those letters that told the whole story,
That were the story.

I can't make it simpler than that.
If they both listen hard, continents apart
They can hear each other's pens scratching.

If they both look, weeks apart,
They can see the paper being folded.
I'm trying to make it simple
But the myth shoulders in
Like a drunk in a pub.

Okay, let it be the myth.
Listen to the scratching.
See the paper folding,
Folding.

Somewhere on the South China Sea in 1938

The waves rose and fell like the Lanarkshire hills;
My dad stood on the deck of a ship that pitched
And rolled and thought of Cathkin Park.

Not perfectly flat, but flatter than this.

His dad had told him by his joiner's bench
Of the Argentinian tour the team undertook
Via Cherbourg, Coruna, Vigo and Lisbon in 1923.

Not a perfect year, but better than some.

And maybe that made the link: Third Lanark/
Romance/World Travel and my dad
Signed up for the navy and the endless horizons.

Not a perfect job, but sweeter than many.

And nobody knew how things would turn out:
The war, the future, the long decline of a club
Until the last ball kicked, the last whistle blown.

Not a perfect end, and sadder than most.

But now my dad gazes out at some flying fish
Beautifully low over the South China water, carving the
    space
Like Third Lanark on a perfect Saturday.

Yes, perfect. Just perfect. Cathkin Park perfect.

Tricycle/Auntie's Elbow/Pocket Watch in Church

It's a strange thing, this writing of a life.
You cast your net over the side and see what comes up
Flapping and gasping beside the shopping trolleys
And the plastic bags. That tricycle you tried to launch
To the moon. That morning when you saw your auntie's
     face
Through a star-shaped hole in that holiday bungalow
     window
In Great Yarmouth. That Sunday morning
When the Reverend Wilfrid Howard, bald as a shoe,
Stopped you pretending to hypnotise Noel with a
     swinging watch
By shouting 'We don't hypnotise people in church,
     laddie!'
Why do these get landed and bashed with the priest
And put into the bag to take home? Why not that time
     that bloke
Knocked on the door when you were watching
Alfred Hitchcock's *Lifeboat* and asked if he could have
A bowl of water for his dog? No significance, I suppose.
No resonance. Nothing to build on. Nothing to grasp.
But, oh, that star-shaped hole! Oh, that swinging watch!
Oh, that tricycle achieving escape velocity!

Every Other Thursday

Every other Thursday the front room
Would be alive with two smells: that hairdresser
Aroma, and the brown paper that the comics came in.
The *Victor*, the *Valiant*, the *Beano*, the *Dandy*
And what my mother called A Commando Book,

Brought back from Great Houghton on the bumping 37,
The air blue with smoke and coughing and words
That the Tough of the Track didn't say. Well, not
In the *Victor*, anyway. Maybe he said them at home
In the house he shared with Flapper Farmer

Where they dressed as pirates. Girl Pirates.
Girl pirates with banjos singing cowboy songs
Late into the night. 'Mexicali Rose': that was the one
My dad liked to croon as he washed up. Those comics
In that brown paper led me to these
Words on this page. It's as simple as that.

NCB Recruiting Film, 1964

They've taken us into the boys' cloakroom to watch it;
It was the darkest place they could find; well, it always was
For David Rotherham.

At one end Mr Challenger fiddled with the projector;
Suddenly the music started and a vicarish voice
Began the story.

The nation needs coal and the nation needs miners.
And, decades later, I wonder why they didn't bother
To move the coats

So that the pitmen moved and shimmered over
     gaberdines
And duffels and macs, spare pegs sticking from their snap
     tins,
Helmets lighting a scarf.

The projector kept speeding up and slowing down,
     smoking
And gasping at its own smoke. Mr Challenger clipped it
And it raced itself

To a finishing line that none of us could guess, the voice
Mickey-mousing and the pitmen running, running,
To a place of sudden darkness.

Great-Aunt Bella and the Wartime Postal System and the West Riding and Rob Brown

If this is an acceptance speech, then these are the ones to
    thank:
Great-Aunt Bella Howatson, who wrote rhyming letters to
    my dad
That he read slowly, leaning over that great dull stone
    sink
At Falla Cottage. If rhyme is in your DNA, then I'm very
    glad
To say she put it there.

And can I thank that wartime postal system, chugging
    those letters
Across continents and seas that boiled and sprayed and
    heaved
And took words and lines from those young seasick lovers
And scattered them across their lives like tumbling leaves,
Leaves that fall through the years.

And can I thank the West Riding of Yorkshire and Sir
    Alec Clegg
Who taught me we are all creative, and that a playground
    game
Leads straight to Shakespeare and that the harsh sound
    of a clog

Can echo through your veins until it holds you like a
   rhyme
That you remember as you dance.

And can I thank Rob Brown, English teacher in a green
   suit
Who told me that it was okay to try to become a poet,
That even though my voice was more a theremin than a
   flute
I had something inside me. And I should try to grow it,
Even if the growing made it coarser.

Andy and Sandie

My dad loved to sing. His sweet tenor voice
Filled UHE 8 those long Sunday afternoons
Between home and Brierley Crossroads, Houghton Woods
And the slow road home in third trundle gear
As my dad sang like Andy Stewart

Or Sandie Shaw. 'Donald, Where's Yer Troosers?'
And 'Puppet on a String' over and over, looping
And dancing as that bright blue car
Passed the house where he told us Dick Turpin lived
'with his horse Black Beauty'.

The songs shrank: over the years they became
Small photographs of themselves. Just the first line,
Just the first couple of words. 'I've just ...' 'I wonder ...'
Because we all knew the rest, the rhythms living
In our souls like the route home.

And then you shrank. That bastard stroke
Sat you in the chair and wouldn't let you get up
To change the channels on the television
As the carers came and went like Sunday afternoons
But somewhere in there you were singing.

The Thames-Clyde Express

21/05/64

A trainspotter's notebook and a pencil
Taken from school. The mates, the ones
Who said I would see the most amazing engines
As they slowed down past the turn in the bridle path
By Houghton Main pit.

The grass was making me sneeze, so understand
This: everything that follows is an impression,
Something seen through frosted glass, maybe
Something I never really saw, just imagined
Then wrote down with my pencil.

The Thames-Clyde express, on its long way north,
Slows almost to a stop, and a restaurant car
Packed with toffs is tucking in to something
Served by a chef in a sculpted hat, brandishing
A spoon that shines.

We waved. We waved our notebooks and pencils
As behind the train the pit wheels turned
As a shift came up or went down. A man in a suit
Turned to us with a face like a half-dead balloon,
Lifted two fuckoff fingers high in the air.

Speyk

'Sees. Tha noz. Tha wants to frame thissen.
Geeor rooarin when they org thee on.
They dun't mean it. They're just messin
And him doing rawpin's no moor than four ston
Wet through. Streeak o' pump watter.
Owt they seh to thee dun't matter.'

Thanks, Uncle Charlie. Thanks for them words
And the love behind 'em, the love unheard
Much of the time behind the rattling of the chest.
Good men and better men, Charlie. You were the best.

The New Library, April 1964

We walked up there in a classful, talking all the way
Up Snape Hill. Somebody's mam
Was hanging vast white pants on a washing line,
And we waved to her. We all had green tickets
And I was hoping for Biggles, praying for Biggles.

She waved back. A shirt hung on the line like a ghost
That knew something about the future that we didn't.
We waved our green tickets like they were important.
'Biggles Flies Open' Robert Doughty said. Peter Wake
    laughed
But I didn't get it. I'd not heard of that one,

Maybe it would be there, in the new library. The mam
    waved
Again, and the pants waved, and the shirt waved
And the green tickets waved. 'Biggles Has Flies in his
    Sarnies'
Peter Wake said. Mrs Roche said 'Right, stop waving now!'
But we were waving to welcome something,

And waving goodbye to something else;
Something I'm only just beginning to be able to spell.

Adult Fiction

I always loved libraries, the quiet of them,
The smell of the plastic covers and the paper
And the tables and the silence of them,
The silence of them that if you listened wasn't silence,
It was the murmur of stories held for years on shelves
And the soft clicking of the date stamp,
The soft clickety-clicking of the date stamp.

I used to go down to our little library on a Friday night
In late summer, just as autumn was thinking about
Turning up, and the light outside would be the colour
Of an Everyman cover and the lights in the library
Would be soft as anything, and I'd sit at a table
And flick through a book and fall in love
With the turning of the leaves, the turning of the leaves.

And then at seven o'clock Mrs Dove would say
In a voice that wasn't too loud so it wouldn't
Disturb the books 'Seven o'clock please ...'
And as I was the only one in the library's late summer
    rooms
I would be the only one to stand up and close my book
And put it back on the shelf with a sound like a kiss,
Back on the shelf with a sound like a kiss.

And I'd go out of the library and Mrs Dove would stand
For a moment silhouetted by the Adult Fiction,
And then she would turn the light off and lock the door
And go to her little car and drive off into the night
That was slowly turning the colour of ink and I would
      stand
For two minutes and then I'd walk over to the dark
      library
And just stand in front of the dark library.

Dam Flask Days, 1965

It's raining. People say that in their memories of childhood it's always sunny but not in this memory. The rain is stair rods. My dad and my Uncle Jack have taken me fishing. They like the rain and the dark, dark sky.

Better than work my dad says, and for some reason he's laughing so much he's crying. Uncle Jack is cracking eggs into a cup and adding brandy. Uncle Jack fought in the war and he remembers General Mark Clark driving past him in a jeep in the desert. My dad fought in the war and he remembers carrying naked sailors back from brothels through the streets of Shanghai.

But let them enjoy their eggs in the rain.

Folk Tale: The Owl in the Tower, 1966

Gather on Barnsley Road, walk down School Street,
Run from the Cross Keys with beer wings on your feet
Stand round the church in the darkening hour
And talk of the thing that's the Owl in the Tower

Theer. Did tha see it? Flash o' white theer.
It screeches tha noz; tha can hear its wings flappin
And a cross between a door squeakin and a dog yappin
And tha shivers wi summat thaz got to call Fear.

Feel the tale grow as you stand in the dark
As others creep in from the gloom of the park
Stand round the church in the darkening hour
And watch for the horror: the Owl in the Tower

It took a babby straight from its pram
Pecked a kid in't throit who tried to stop it
Took it reyt up to't tower top and dropped it
Straight into't arms on its open-gobbed mam.

The tale grows in the telling, filling the spaces,
Lighting the darkness and lighting the faces
Stand round the church in the darkening hour
And wait for the horror: the Owl in the Tower

Thez two on em. At least. Tha calls it an owl
But I call it three beeasts, three beeasts wi wings
Wi beaks that can slash thi and claws that can sting
A bird of destruction, a ghooast devil fowl . . .

After midnight they're still there, straining to hear
As their breath turns to mist and the clouds start to clear;
Stand round the church in the darkening hour
And hope for the horror: the Owl in the Tower.

In the Queue at the Ballachulish Ferry: Colours and Sounds

UHE 8 (*blue*) limps forward like the rest of them
On this *grey* day in the Highlands. Midges
Scribble on the air and my brother (*blonde*) sits in the
    back

Endlessly singing the phrase 'Boats are going by.'
'There's something wrong with the ferry'
My dad (*grey*) says, climbing back in. A busker appears

Suddenly, in the window, making my mother jump.
Boats are going by. He (*grey*) beckons to me (*blonde*)
And I climb out of the car (*blue*) and the midges dance
    on my face

(*red*). He holds the violin (*brown*) and I hold the bow.
He moves the violin as I hold the bow. Music happens
(*many colours. Some of them strange*). Boats are going by.

He takes the bow and gives me the violin (*brown*)
And I stand still and he moves the bow. Music happens
(*many colours. Some of them strange*). No conclusion,
    really,

This close to the end of the poem. Something about
    music,
And colour, and making music, and vivid colours in
    greyness,
And my dad passing him a bob (*silver*).

Violin

It's early spring 1971 and the nights are lightening.
Look: here at the bus-stop, Ian and Steve, waiting.
Practice went well says Steve. Ian says
The gig should be good. That word *gig*
Feels funny in his mouth like sherry or raw fish.

A bus pulls round the corner in slow motion
And Steve steps forward raising his hand.
Tuesday same time he says. Ian says
Nothing because worlds are about to collide
This evening at the edge of a new decade.

The bus door opens and Steve climbs on;
He's painted a frog on his violin case
Because the band's name is Oscar the Frog
And the bus isn't the Barnsley bus,
It's the pit bus from Houghton Main.

Oh, just pause and imagine it. The frog.
The violin case. The pitmen straight off afters.
The hooting. The laughter. The *Give us a tune
Paganinny.* The *Tha's a funny snap tin theer.*
The long high keening note, the scraping.

First Gig

The curtains creak open so this must be showbiz
But the jumble sale has already begun so maybe it isn't.
At the Church Hall the wall heaters glow faintly red
And people like Mrs McCardle and Freda Crofts
Look up briefly like you might glance at a passing plane.

We don't care; a nod from Martyn and we're off
Into 'Walk Awhile', that Fairport Convention song
You could file under 'jaunty'. I drum as fast as I can,
Faster than they're playing, faster than those women
Can possibly buy. A kid holds up a ray gun

And pretends to zap us. Yes, fair enough,
But that used to be my ray gun. As each song ends
To no applause we lurch into the next one
Until Roland McCardle, after a nod from the rector,
Hauls the curtains shut like he's hauling in the sails

On a ship that nobody noticed was sinking.
I'm sweating. I throw one of my drumsticks at the curtains
Hoping it'll kill the lad with my ray gun. The rector
Comes backstage and says Well Done but
Even as he's saying it he's backing away.

Nobel Prize

We can all point to one teacher, one wise person
Who opened doors and pointed the way through.
Please welcome Mr Brown. Please welcome his corduroy
    suit.
Please welcome his beard. Please welcome the
    paperbacks
He kept in the jacket pocket of his green corduroy suit.

He had a beard that preceded him into the classroom.
I can't emphasise enough how rare beards were
In South Yorkshire in the early 1970s. Years later he told
    me
That when he first walked down the main street of Wath
A man in a cap stopped him and said '*What's tha keep in
    theer,*

Pigeons else ferrets?' Which delighted Mr Brown,
Which had stayed with him through the decades.
He encouraged me: showed me poems by Ted Hughes,
Shared his enthusiasms; George Mackay Brown, the
    blues,
Put me on the editorial committee of the school
    magazine,

But when I handed in an essay signed 'Ian McMillan,
Future Nobel Prize For Literature Winner', took me aside
And pointed out (the sun making each wiry hair on his
    beard
Shine like a kind of bohemian City-Lights-Bookstore
    gold)
That Nobel Prize winners didn't come from Barnsley.
    Never would.

There was a moment of silence. Shared silence. Steve
Cameron came in and asked if he could practise his cello.
We let him, Mr Brown and I. We held a corduroy/blazer
    tableau
For long minutes as the sun lit us and Steve's improvised
    notes
Held us still. Really still. Very still. Listen: we are
    breathing.

Please Send More, 1971

I typed the poems out, slowly, starting ag
Starting again if I got a word wrong. I got
The cardboard out of one of my dad's new shirts
And slotted it carefully into the envv
Into the envelope.

I got the cardboard out of another shirt
And slotted it carefully into the envelope.
I slid the poems, all six of them with my name and
    address
Across the top, into the envelope
Between the cardboard.

I stuck the stamp on the stamped addressed envelope
And banged it down with my fust
And banged it down with my fist.
I folded the covering letter *I enclose*
Six of my poems for your consideration.

I have had poems published in Contac
And Roots. I enclose a tamped a stamped
Addressed envelope. Peace, Ian McMillan.
Mr Alderson at the Post Office looked cynical
When I went in. 'More masterpieces?' he said.

'More shirts?' I'd made the mistake
Of telling him about the shirts, about the
Carboard about the cardboard from the shirts.
I touched the envelope before it went,
Trying to give it some kind of blessing.

Under Fourteens

Mr Fisher grabbed me by the shoulder
And said, in his surprisingly high voice,
'This is swearing, McMillan,
But I think you've got the arse for rugby!'

I reddened and nodded and he put me in the scrum,
To face Ecclesfield Grammar on a freezing morning
Just after Jimi Hendrix had died alone in a room
And a scrum is a kind of room. Unfurnished, with
Just the natural light of sun filtered through
Shirts and bad, bad words. And that's swearing.

Mr Fisher shouted from the touchline
In his choirman's tenor: 'Power, McMillan,
Power!' And I could sense my dad wincing
Even in that room with its shirty walls.

I tried to shove and came up against a wall
And a kid who was supposed to be thirteen
Poked me in the eye and called me a twat
And that's swearing. I wanted to escape to a place
Where I could read books and discuss Ted Hughes
Wittily, making references to an older tradition

And he was gouging my eye like he was trying
To get a whelk out of its shell. I felt myself squeezed

Upwards. I heard Mr Fisher shout 'McMillan,
Where the hell are you going?' and I saw my dad's
Trilby and his scarf and his raised hands
And I think Ted Hughes' 'Pike' is an interesting

Example of what you might call a New Nature Poetry.
I shot out of the scrum-room upwards like a salmon
And fell in a heap as the ball and the shorts ran away up
The grass. My neck hurt. My neck really hurt.
My neck really bloody bastard hurt and that's swearing
Of a high order. My dad ran on to the field and I was
     crying.

Later, Dr Scott sat me on a chair in his surgery
That was a room made of pain and tears and said
'This might hurt. Think about something else.'
So I thought about Emma Peel and he lifted me

Up by my head and I heard my neck click.
I heard it go like this: click. It clicked.

The Eye Blinked./It/Watered: Wales and Barnsley, 1973

On a field trip to Barmouth, steeped in Ted Hughes
And R. S. Thomas, and scribbling in the shared room,
I saw the poet I thought I might become:
In a suit, late at night, with a pen.

After the rattling bus took us high into the hills
And we saw a *Cwm* shining in late afternoon sun
I tried to write on the back seat; my head spun
And Mr Hinchcliffe told me to breathe and look out of
the window.

Back at home, listening to *Valentyne Suite* by Colosseum
On the Dansette, with my dad saying 'What's that row?'
I wrote three lines that seemed to me then to be a poem:
The eye blinked./It/Watered. I set it out like this

The eye blinked.
It
Watered.

I showed it to Mr Brown in English who said
It had a kind of haiku quality. I smiled
But I didn't know what a haiku was. Mr Brown
Suggested a tiny change to 'The eye blinked./It watered.'

He called it a mature example of my work.
I was seventeen. All young poets should have
A man like Mr Brown to wave their early words at.
A haiku quality. A haiku quality. A haiku quality.

Somewhere on a Back Lane
Near Oxford in 1976

The minibus has stopped. The night is clear.
Five sweating students are pissing beer
Against the tyres.

One turns to another and simply smiles
Because he can, now that there's Oxford miles
Between them and it.

John Morris is the first to speak
And his voice is shaken, stumbling, weak:
'That was the future

Boys. The whole of music's changed
And the map's been redrawn, rearranged;
Now Punk has come.'

We nodded sagely; undergrads
Let loose from doting mams and dads
To study politics.

We'd been to Oxford to see three bands
To experience and understand
This brand-new scene.

The Tyla Gang, The Vibrators
And top of the bill, The Stranglers
Scared us to death.

Noisy aggressive two-minute blasts
Defined the future, shat on the past
And Dave Thorpe said

In his slow and careful Newark voice
'Having seen that, if you gave me a choice
I'd come again.'

We thought we were so bloody smart
Like a donkey who learns if he pulls the cart
The cart will move.

Above us the timeless stars just shone
On five kids with army greatcoats on:
Let's leave them there,

Sweating and glowing with a kind of light
From being part of something that Tuesday night
They couldn't fathom.

And it's easy to mock from the distance of years
But pardon me for shedding grey-haired tears
For the boy I was.

Hollywood Nights, 1977

After three days on the Greyhound bus
We're glad of a hotel room. We'd saved up
The dollars until Hollywood,

Sat on the bus with the man called
Curlers who stood up to announce
To everyone that 'these guys are English

And that means they drink warm brown beer!'
To scattered applause, and the postman
From the Bronx who said 'I moved. They were

Burning the blocks. Block after block.
Block after block. I had to skedaddle.'
He took my nod for assent not tiredness

And as we sat in a bus station in Phoenix
He said 'Hey, English: up there in the mountains
It's cool as a freezer but down here

It'll burn your balls off. It's not like this in England,
Is it?' He was right there. Me, Bob Allen, Dave Thorpe:
Three kids scared and exhilarated on a 90-dollar

Unlimited Greyhound pass. So we rolled into LA, got a
    taxi
To a motel in Hollywood, signed in,
And the man behind the desk, thick glasses like Peter
    Glaze,

Said 'Barnsley, eh? They have a good soccer team, no?'
'Not bad' I said, desperate for sleep. 'I myself support the
Preston North Ends' he said, gesturing to a flag on the
    wall

Behind his desk. Welcome to the American Dream,
Building itself block by block. Later, I had a T-shirt
    printed
With the words 'I HAVE SEEN EVENING CLOUDS

LOOM OVER ARIZONA.' It's a poem, I said to the
    unimpressed
Man at the printing machine. 'Poems rhyme' he said.
'Where's Deepdale?' I said. Only Dave Thorpe laughed.

The Worst Gig Ever, June 1979

I won't name the pub because they might come and
    get me
But I'll tell you this: they were expecting heavy metal
Not two lads with beards and poems and stories.
I should have known when the landlord said 'Evening
    petal,

Back your van up to the door' and I said we had no
    van
And he said 'Where's your equipment then, sonny?'
And I had to confess our equipment was two watering
    cans.
Plastic ones. He was fat and he wobbled: 'Are you
    being funny?'

We weren't. And it wasn't. Row after row in black
    leather
Staring and staring. The juke box switched off for the
    night.
Us standing there. With watering cans. You know how
    a feather
Feels before it's plucked from the bird? No? It feels
    like shite.

And that's how it felt. The landlord, from behind the bar,
     stared.
The watering cans were for 'Stranger on the Shore'
The old Acker Bilk hit. It was a bit surreal, it could be
     compared
to Fluxus or anti-art. Or having your balls nailed to the
     floor.

Bilk's finest hour drifted slowly across the smoky lounge
As we blew the cans and the fans of heavy metal booed;
I looked up from blowing and I saw the landlord cringe
And our goose was cooked. Our goose was fried. And
     stewed.

We stopped and the booing reached a deep bass peak.
We left the stage; the landlord sneaked us out
Through a side room. I was almost crying. My legs felt
     weak
And I was sweating like a sprinter and gasping like a
     trout.

And the final insult as the landlord pushed us through
     the door:
'I loved that tune, you know, I've always been a fan of
     Bilk
But you lads killed it. I'll never listen to it any more.'
And we fell into the lonely night, the moon as pale as
     milk.

The Back of My Neck

The barber's is full. Bing Crossley is telling the tale
Of how he once sang 'Three Coins in a Fountain'
In front of the Mayor of Barnsley, who joined in
The chorus and who, according to Bing,
'Had a voice like shot shit'.

Geoff has almost finished 'tidying me up'
As he calls it. I never comb my hair, just let it sprout
Up towards heaven. Bing starts to croon
And Geoff rolls his eyes. Three coins in the fountain,
Three coins in the fountain.

Geoff's done. The song's done. There's applause
From the old pitmen and young lads filling the seats.
Geoff shows me the back of my neck in a mirror
And time stops like a stopped song. The back of my neck
Is the back of his neck.

My dad's neck, looking at me from the mirror
As Geoff flicks grey fog from my loud shirt
And Bing stands up to bow, milking the room
And in the mirror I'm turning into my father.
And behind the mirror the ocean rolls.

Degree

They used to set fire to my *Guardian* in the cabin;
It was funny for the first three weeks. I laughed
Like this: ha ha.

'Tha reads heavy, dun't tha?' Cyril said.
You could see his wellies from space.
'We'll call thi *degree* cos tha's got a *degree*'

He said. Arthur nodded. Crackerjack smashed his shovel
On the floor in a kind of agreement. Vinny took off his hat
And pointed to his domed head.

'Nowt theer. Nowt theer, *degree*. Nowt theer.'
The site was muddy; you could lose stuff: boots, hats,
Reputations, maybe. Reading heavy.

'I bet tha clever aren't tha?' Cyril said.
I mumbled something. 'No, no. Tha must be clever
Cos tha's got a *degree*.' He made it sound like a boil.

Walking down to the footings on a dirty morning
I saw Cyril up to his thighs in mud, sinking
Like Carver Doone or the *Titanic*.

'Help! *Degree!* Help me!' he shouted,
His voice hanging in the half-built air
As he continued to sink like a Cyril-shaped stone.

I ran up the site. 'Bloke sinking!' I shouted
And they all came running: Arthur, Crackerjack,
Ted, Vinny; the tractor driver drove his tractor down

And I knew this was the last time I'd
Scan a charred *Guardian*, the last time
I'd hide my Kerouac in my snap bag.

We gathered round Cyril. We were like a ritual.
Mud people gathered round a sinking mud-man.
We made a circle and the sun broke through a cloud

And for a second I glowed in its promise.
Then Cyril stood up, slowly; slow as the flames
That licked my liberal left-leaning broadsheet.

It reddens my cheeks now, decades on.
Obvious, really: he'd just been kneeling in the mud.
Everyone clapped except me.

'Not so clever, are tha, *degree?*'
Cyril said. I felt the flames beginning to take hold
Of my old college jeans. The smoke made my eyes water.

At the Tennis Ball Factory, 1980

The rubber dust moved like water in the bobbling
barrow. If you volunteered for overtime that was one of
the things they gave you to do: take the rubber dust out
and bury it at the back.

Alan, who once made his own false teeth, had a
barrowful too. 'You can't call this work, can you?' he said.

His mate Barry agreed. 'It's not a job, this.'

Now the factory is gone and there's an estate of
houses there called Tuscan Gardens, because Barnsley is
the new Tuscany, and as I go by and the wind is strong
and the cars are shaking the road, I can see the estate
moving, bouncing gently.

Workshop Days, 1981/83

There was the one who turned up in full Highland rig,
His *skean dhu* glinting in the pale library light.
There was the one who arrived with two broken arms,
Rapped his pot on the door as he came in.
There was the one who jumped headlong into the
    pantoum,
Each week writing more and more: *Tha just has to write*
Half as much as tha needs, kid! he'd say, triumphant.
The one who sat taking an age to write one letter
Then looked at us looking at him and clicked the pen
And stuffed it back in his pocket and said, in a thin voice
A bit like a kid's first lesson on the violin, *Not calligraphy,*
    then?
There was the one who sat silent then asked a question
Right at the end as we were stacking the chairs:
I only came here to learn one thing; you've not really covered it.
We stopped stacking the chairs; outside I saw my 226
    rumble by,
Which meant I'd have another half an hour to wait in the
    raw night.
He pulled a book from his Co-op carrier. I could see that
    he'd
Typed it himself and bound it with sellotape. *Can tha just*
    tell me

What kind of glue tha should use? To bind it, I mean?
There was the one who wrote exquisite verse of love and
    romance
Then always excused himself by saying *I've got to get off;*
I've a parcel of Nazi torture videos coming. There was the one
Who cycled all the way from Monk Fryston, arrived
    sweating,
Glugged water from a flask, crunched biscuits for energy,
    then sat
And listened. Never read a poem or a story, just listened.
    If I tried
To make comments on the piece we'd just heard, he'd
    raise a hand
And stop me. After all these years I remember his hand
    was hairy.
No, Ian. No, lad. That was beautiful, simply beautiful.
I'll tell you what: I'd like to sit in a big armchair
With a glass of whisky and listen to that one again.
I was silent and I sulked. Some weeks he didn't come
And I was in charge again. But when he came, sweating,
    hairy,
He reduced his keynote speech to a couple of words:
Armchair. Whisky. And the others nodded. They nodded
And they murmured. And I looked out of the window
And saw another 226 going by. Each week, in libraries and
Meeting rooms all across South Yorkshire in lean and
    cracking years
I encouraged them all. The fact is, I loved them. And I
    still do:

The ones who try to write, the ones who won't be told
    they can't,
The ones who believe that they can write just as well
As the ones they see on the shelves. The ones who splash
Into pantoums like they are splashing into a sea that
    never ends.

Heart of Darkness, 1984

Early morning, as I walk to Wombwell Station, I hear it:
A shout of 'scab!' from the lane that leads to Darfield
    Main
And I know that things are crumbling. A police van, and
    another,
Rumble by; I've heard the rumour they are full of
    soldiers

And I believe it. They turn on their sirens and their lights
Just to wake everybody up, just because they can, and the
    sky
Cracks a little to let in a line of light that will become
    today
And I turn my collar up against the wind that feels colder

Than ever, now that it's blowing from the future, from
The Call Centres and the broken Community Centre
    windows
And the minimum wage jobs that crack you a little more
    each day
But let in no light, no light.

Another Bad Gig: High Ham, 1988

All week on this village hall tour of Somerset people have been saying to us *If you think tonight's gig is good wait till you get to High Ham . . .*

High Ham. The name resonates and sings. The night before the High Ham show we go to Evensong at Wells Cathedral and the voices articulate the light.

High Ham. The poster outside the village hall is in vivid red letters. An articulation of light. TONIGHT: YAKETY YAK! ADULT COMEDIANS! The exclamation marks are slaps in the chops.

At this distance I might be making the organiser's beard up. I told him we weren't adult comedians. Told him we were daft lads telling daft stories. He said we'd be okay. His beard moved.

We stood there. Our words refused to articulate the light. After nearly an hour of the kind of silence you could hang in a gallery a man comes to the front and says *I'm going to the toilet now; if you say something funny while I'm out let me know.*

Imagine the rest, if you like.

Partially Overheard, Partially Invented: Darfield, 1985/2007

Seez, some on 'em were rooarin an blutherin
Ther soul-cases art but A sez 'No; lerrem shut.
Lerrem shut darn. Would tha gu darn theer?'
A sez to one kid wi a banner. 'No, tha wun't.'

An e sez to me 'But what tha gunner put theer instead?'
An A sez 'They'll see thi or8. Nubdy's gunner let thi rot!'
An then cos this is a poem tha can fast forward to't future,
An A wish A'd not. Wheer number 2 shaft wo'

Tha can buy beeans else soup. An A saw a kid stacking
An A sez 'Are thy a Gibson?' E sez 'R.' A sez 'Tha looks
    like thi dad.'
An e sez 'Am glad A dun't sarnd like the twat' and then
    cos
This is a poem A woh sat next to Bill in his bed

An iz belluses had gone. Sarnded like scrapin. Sarnded
    like
A kid runnin darn a shingle beach. Sarnded like he wo'
Tranna bring summat up. 'What tha tranner bring up?'
A sez to him. And cos this is a poem e turnz to mi
Wi' a face that looks like meltin ice an e sez 'Istri!'

Just Like Watching Brazil, April 1997

You can always guess the end of a film or a play;
The unlikely suspect killed the girl, the lovers stand and
   kiss
But this outcome, on this drizzling April day?
They'd think you were taking the piss.

I think that art should be much more like sport;
The real-time endeavour and the drama and the farce
As the try's put down, the sky-high ball is caught
And the showoff falls on his arse.

But today art and sport combine and come together
In Clint Marcelle's sublime goal that lifts this northern
   town
Beyond the boot of history and this day's shitty weather
And we know we'll never come down.

(Until the relegation bell rings loud down shattered
   streets
And the town reflects that history's just a cycle of
   defeats.)

Song of Stanage Edge and My Dad's Old Hat

The stone that looks like a nose
Breathes it all in:
The wind's knife, the sky's bowl,
And the cloud shaped like my dad's old hat
Sailing towards me like he sailed home.

Come and sit here with me, Dad
At Stanage Edge on this blue day
And we'll talk about the view.
Sit here, Dad. I miss you.

The sky stepped back into cloud
And the folding horizon was kissed by haze.
A man in camouflage pants
Bounded out from behind the stone
Pulled by a dog as white as milk.

And up here it all feels timeless:
That cloud could be a white dog,
That stone still looks like a nose;
And you taught me to walk, Dad,
And you taught me to look.

Come and sit here with me, Dad
Here at Stanage Edge on this blue day.
And we'll talk about the view.
Sit here, Dad. I miss you.

Two Pyjama Incidents

1.

1964. Pulled from sleep in night's dark core
To sit with our John and my dad
And watch Cassius Clay and Sonny Liston
On that telly that sat in the corner of everything.

Hard to explain, but what I remember most
Is my surprise that the furniture was still there;
The settee, fatly, the cage with Dicky in it
His eyes bright even at this time, the wall lights
That looked like shells.

And my dad's dressing gown. Paisley. A belt.

2.

1969. David Frost is telling me
And our John and my dad
That people have landed on the moon.
Dicky's not there, but the shells are.
Still washed up on the wall's beach.

And my dad's dressing gown. A belt. Paisley.

Talking Myself Home

I'm under a table in a small hotel in Plymouth in 1958,
And I'm talking. Someone says, in a loud voice,
Some day that boy will be prime minister. I'm in Harry
   Holden's
Barber's in Darfield in 1963 and I'm talking, talking.

I'm asking anyone in the stuffed room how you can get
   jewels
Into a watch. *Moor rattle than a can o mabs* says Harry,
Rubbing Brylcreem into Mr Snowball's quiff. I'm asking
Mr Fleming-Smith about the origin of deck quoits

And he says *Just stop talking, talking, talking, McMillan*
And it must be a kind of nervousness that makes him
   repeat
The word; after all, it's 1968 and the world is exploding.
I'm talking to Dave Thorpe about the way the sax solo

In Baker Street actually can define, actually define, the
   world
Better than, say Ginsberg or Wittgenstein. I should really
   be
Reading up for tomorrow's seminar. It's 1976 and I'm
Talking, talking, talking, talking. Dave Thorpe, his sensible

Newark voice rolling round his flat like the dropped top
Of a brown sauce bottle, says *Just stop a minute, Mac:*
Let the room breathe. It's 1985 and I'm pushing ten pences
Into a phone box at Barnsley General; upstairs Elizabeth
    is saying

Hello to the world and I'm talking, talking, talking,
    talking,
Talking and my mother is saying *Slow down a bit! Are they*
Both okay? It's 1993 and I'm in front of a crowd
    somewhere
Or everywhere and they're saying *Hey this kid is good*

Well, I'm making that up; I'm good at talking, talking,
Talking, talking, talking, talking, you see. I begin to read
Another poem, then another. I've got new ones here
And new ones in my head unwritten, unread. It's 2004

And I'm cradling my grandson in my arms; it's snowing
Outside and I'm telling him it's snowing. *Welcome,* I say;
Let me talk you home. Snowing words, Thomas. Talking
Talking, talking, talking, talking, talking, talking.

You Wouldn't Want to be in This Book

I know you wouldn't want to be in this book,
Like you don't want to be on photos;
I know you'd say that such as this book wasn't for you
But it is.

Geological Shifts; A Poem that Shifts into Prose as Pieces Fall Off

Living in the same place all this time
You notice things changing slowly, slowly.
For years a carrier bag hung on a wire near our house;
Over the weeks and the months and the seasons
It shredded in a slow gentle way, flakes of carrier-bag snow
Tumbling down late at night when nobody was looking,
Until one handle remained, getting smaller, smaller
Until I really had to look to see it. As the bag changed,
The world changed. My hair went grey. The kids grew up
And one by one left home. My mother and father died
And I carried on cracking my knuckles annoyingly
And clearing my throat. Every few years my wife would say
    to me
'Stop cracking your knuckles and clearing your throat'
But I would take no notice. On the window sill in the
    kitchen
There's a pebble shaped like a shark's head that
I took from a beach in Northumberland in, when, 1988,
    1989,
And there's a tile that we stand the teapot on that I took
from a disused church in 1980 or 1981 and the teapot has
been standing on it for nearly thirty years and when I stay
in hotels or go to conferences I like to get the free pens
or notebooks because they might come in handy and the

other day as I was looking for a pen the whole lot tumbled out of the cupboard like bits of carrier bag falling from a wire and I found a notebook that I'd got from a library in Cheshire in 1984. I cracked my knuckles and cleared my throat.

Three

There you are, the three of you, on a beach somewhere.
It's cold, look. You're huddled together, close together.
Remember that coat? Remember that hat? That scarf?
I'm not on the photo and your mother's taking it. Listen:
Click.

I used to put poems in your lunchboxes. Your mates
Thought we didn't have a telly and we sat in a circle
Reading to each other and then, instead of clapping
We'd raise our arms and snap our fingers. Listen:
Snap.

I just like looking at the photo albums. Remember this?
When you ran down that same beach until I could hardly,
Yes, there you are, just, see you. It's a photo of a beach
    really.
With three figures there in the distance, laughing. Listen:
I know. I know they're only photos. But we can still hear
    you.

Available Light

Early morning, the security light comes on as next door
    Gillian
In her nightie goes out to throw bread that hangs briefly in
    the air
Like feathers. Moon still there, waiting to wane.
Lights of a plane coming down to Leeds/Bradford; paper
    lad's
Bike light as he stops outside Mrs Fisher's. Security light goes
    off
And I remember: floodlights fighting the fog at Oakwell,
Trying to read in a tent with the light of a watch with a lit-up
    face,
Blue lights of coppers leading a van with grills for windows
Back to the pit whose orange lights seemed hard
In the February dark, light coming through the smashed
    window
And reflecting on the glass shards as I turn the key on the
    inside
As I break in to find my mother on the floor, harsh hospital
    lights
Where I first held my children and my grandson and
Next door's security light flicks off; in its afterglow the shirt
On Gillian's line waves like a ghost, a ghost defined by light
Like we all are.

Slipstream

Yes, but if everybody can write and sing and perform
    and dance,
Then who will the audience be? Where will they all
    sit?

Will they have to crowd into one small room?
    Everyone
Will have booklets and CDs and cards with their
    MySpace page

On them and they'll want to give them out. Where
    will they all sit?
But if everybody can write and sing and perform and
    dance

Then I have to read all their books and listen to all
    their CDs
And what about the fact that everybody can paint and
    when

Will I find the Lemon and Lime (rhyming slang.
    Yeeha!)
To look and listen and watch and hear and see and
    smell?

But if I'm serious about this, about the idea that we can
   all do it,
Then I have to acknowledge that we all can. So, this is my
   life

But this is your work. Discuss.

Speyk 2

Tha noz speykin comes hard to them at's been teld
Their speykin grates like fingernails darn glass.
And if theer's a body of knowledge tha noz the bugger's
   held
Somewheer wheer them as speyks like this can't pass.

But it seems to me that speykin's not a sport
That some can win while others simply fail
Tha chucks the words and then the words get caught;
And the corncrake can sing just like the nightingale.

Remembering

A handful of stars
And one round medal
And the polish.

No war stories
Just the polish
And the stars.

November rain
And the television
And the tears.

One round medal:
Just a coin
That can't be spent.

And the stars
And no war stories
And the polish.

Back from the Tunnels

I came back from filming tunnels under Wakefield Town
    Hall
To my parents' house where we always went for Saturday
    tea
To find my dad slumped and silent against the bedroom
    wall
His legs had given way and his eyes were back at sea;
Downstairs the kids were chewing through the tableful
    my mother
Set each week at this time; food is love. The sarnies and
    pork pies
And then the melons cut in boats and 'Just make room
    for another
Trifle, will you, and move that plate.' Upstairs he half-sits,
    half-lies
And we wait for the doctor to come through the gate.
    'No trouble'
He says. 'No trouble at all.' Dad, I should have rung the
    ambulance
And not listened to a stumbling word you tried to say,
    then said
As your big hands fluttered in a twisted, trembling dance
And the *Ark Royal* sat becalmed in the ocean in your
    head.

I guess I didn't want to admit that things would never be
    the same
As I kept watch for the doctor's car lights trundling down
    the lane.

25/12/01

A nurse with tinsel round her hat stands with us in the lift;
I hesitate at the door of your wheezing room.
As another nurse comes in with a wrapped-up gift
And her bright Tarn voice cuts through the gloom:
'We got him a present; it's just summat we do
At Christmas' and she hands it to me. I walk to your bed.
You're not long for this tired world, Dad; that's true,
And I smooth the grey hair on your beautiful head
As I clutch your present. But please don't slip away
Just yet. I love you just like you loved the sea,
And I don't want to lose you on this Christmas Day.
But I'm not thinking of you. I'm thinking of me,

So go on, Dad. Go now, as the tide starts to turn.
You had so much to teach me. If I'd wanted to learn.

(And the present? Deodorant and aftershave.
Go fragrantly and scented to that Christmas Day grave.)

A Wind Straight from Siberia

At my mother's funeral at the start of a new year the wind
is blowing straight from Siberia. It's been raining and
there are buckets in the old church at Great Houghton
catching the drips.

The old pall bearers are nearly blown away, a white comb-
over
Or two waving like seaweed, and a half-stumble, and a
glance
Between me and Charlesworth that says *Don't drop her. Not
now.*

We needn't have bothered. The wind ignores the men in
dark suits and lifts the coffin in the air and pings off the
lid and there she goes, high in the sky, waving to us all,
laughing again, and wishing, really wishing,

That she'd had her hair done.